Random Thoughts
of a
Simple Mind

(In Twenty Words or Less)

Random Thoughts
of a
Simple Mind

(In Twenty Words or Less)

FRED C. GILMER

iUniverse, Inc.
New York   Bloomington

Random Thoughts of a Simple Mind
(In Twenty Words or Less)

iUniverse books may be ordered through booksellers or by contacting:

iUniverse
1663 Liberty Drive
Bloomington, IN 47403
www.iuniverse.com
1-800-Authors (1-800-288-4677)

Because of the dynamic nature of the Internet, any Web addresses or links contained in this book may have changed since publication and may no longer be valid. The views expressed in this work are solely those of the author and do not necessarily reflect the views of the publisher, and the publisher hereby disclaims any responsibility for them.

ISBN: 978-1-4401-1288-1 (sc)
ISBN: 978-1-4401-1289-8 (ebook)

Library of Congress Control Number: 2009925676

Printed in the United States of America

iUniverse rev. date: 4/17/2009

Contents

Chapter I   For the Love of Love   1

Chapter II   Young and Innocent   27

Chapter III   Heaven and Earth (And all that comes with it)   39

Chapter IV   Trials and Tribulations (But not without hope)   53

Chapter V   Inner Peace (And not so...)   67

Chapter VI   People (The good and the bad)   83

Chapter VII   The Curse of War   97

Chapter VIII   Taboos   103

Chapter IX   Odds and Ends (Leftovers)   121

Foreword

Here's a challenge for you; close your eyes, clear your mind of all thoughts and expectations. Now, open your eyes. What's the first thing you see? Okay, now, quickly, in 20 words or less write a poem about it. Rhyming doesn't matter. Just write without thinking too hard.

Next challenge, pick a word, any word. It could be a person, place, or thing. Or it could be any happening. Again, in 20 words or less, write about it. Any style of poetry will do, Free Verse or otherwise.

Last challenge, try this; pick at most 20 unrelated words at random. Scramble them then unscramble them and try to make sense of them by forming any number of those words, no more than twenty, into a coherent sentence, verse, or poem.

"Random Thoughts of a Simple Mind (In Twenty Words or Less)" is just what this book is about, choosing a few words and making them mean something without trying too hard. Or just pick an object or happening and do the same thing. You will be amazed at what your mind will come up with.

We humans have a very creative mind, if we just let it wander without restricting it or forcing it to do what your conscious mind thinks it should. A lot can be said in just a few words. Greatness may happen.

Preface

"My name is Frederick C. "Jack" Gilmer, Jr."

You can call me Frederick, you can call me Fred, or you can call me Jack, but, please, don't call me Frederick C. "Jack" Gilmer, Jr.

Senseless words end in bore,

Wasted lines flow no more.

Let my feelings show.

Enjoy!

Chapter I

For the Love of Love

True Love

One must endure time alone

To appreciate true love at home.

Rushing River

Rushing river pulling me,

Got to swim away,

Holding onto this tree branch,

Your love found my way.

Blessed Spirit

Enduring love and endless desires,

Eternal dreams of thee.

Refreshing memories of softest eyes,

Your blessed spirit shall be free.

Silken Skin

Your clean, silken skin,

Soft to the touch.

My eyes flirt in silence.

I am drunk with desire.

Trembling Hands

Hands trembling,

Knuckles reaching their whiteness

While remembering her love,

Soft beauty and smoothness.

Robert the Robber

Every night not making love,

My desire for you is over,

Robert cleverly stole your heart.

Robert is a robber.

Logic Interlude

A dream of logic interlude

Is a soul's inaudible desperation

Of burning secret's breathless thoughts

For disclosure of passionate love.

Under Moon and Stars

Perched high above the balcony,

Through jutting, knotted trees,

Moonlight caresses her silky skin,

Starlight finds her eyes.

Life Together

Moonlight passing across

Seamless sand

While stars of night reminds them

Of life together they once planned.

Wings of Love

Soothing words of life's

Wisdom, peace, and joy

Harmoniously soar

On the wings of love.

Lost Love

Dreamt a dream of shorelines,

A story of islands and coastlines,

Watched my love departing,

My joy and companionship fading.

Naughty Laughter

Soft, untethered sunlight

Focused on my True Love so caressed.

Enjoyed her naughty laughter,

I felt unfairly blessed.

In Love and Lonely

In love yet lonely,

Single and still puzzled.

Nearing my twilight years

With my questions gone unanswered.

Nature's Gift

Nature bestowed us

With infinite charm

And soft, subtle laughter.

Smile sometimes

And tell her you love her.

Reconciliation

Unseen sorrow heard,

We could not raise a smile.

Shall we never see tomorrow

'Till we voice it out awhile.

Hot Desire

You inject my soul

With hot desire of you.

Could never end my life

To shed this love so true.

Morning Sunshine

Morning sunshine's caressing light,

Calming walk in Paris,

Soft silky kiss of the sun,

Reminding me of you.

Chapter II

Young and Innocent

Young Innocence

Every child smiling,

Each comforted by love,

Their hearts filled with innocence

And beauty from Heaven above.

The Sound of Children

Illuminated presence

Of assorted impromptu voices

Containing strange informal laughter

And children's joyful noises.

A Child's Heart

A precious child's heart beats

Silently and rhythmically,

With endless love,

Unconditionally.

Ban the Carton

Families torn apart

When a child is lost,

Can't rid ourselves of the pain

By banning all milk cartons.

Learn by Watching

Watching children playing,

Naively imitating grownups,

Toy guns and candy cigarettess,

And dolls they take to spanking.

Dreams of Childhood

Be it one day, a hundred,

Or thousands left,

Be dreaming of my childhood

Until my very death.

Life's Simple Pleasure

Searching for meaning

To life's simple pleasure,

Only to see the smile of a child,

That by which to measure.

My Grand Daughter

Silly little giggles,

A doll named Wiggles,

Two teeth gone,

Sleeps from dusk to dawn.

Wanna see her picture?

Forget Them Not

Raise them in this world

To be good wives and men,

Let us not forget,

For now, they're just children.

Chapter III

Heaven and Earth
(And all that comes with it)

Diversity

Cultural Cornucopia...

Horn of Plenty...

Wealth of Knowledge...

Blades of Grass...

Grains of Sand...

Mass of Humanity...

America the Beautiful

Daylight to Darkness

Shadows of darkness beckoned

O'er gentle rolling meadows,

Trailing the sprinting sun

Across relentless hills.

Romancing the Snow

Enduring the mischievous snow

Yet inspired by its romantic beauty,

Wondrous, sparkling, and alluring glow,

With glistening flakes so silky.

'Tis the Season

Autumn quietly sweeps through woodland trees.

Squirrels gather nuts under fallen leaves,

Preparing for the winter,

For summer is gone.

Where's the Coal

Winter unfurls, turning warm to cold.

My eyes peer through brittle glass,

My bones desire heat.

Where's the coal?

Winter's Cold

Beautiful shade trees' fading colors,

Changing scenes with instant darkness,

Winter season has begun,

Will be cold, could be fun.

Land of Hope

Driving my car across America,

Beautiful land we have here,

Found something, perhaps excitement,

Scenes of hope shone everywhere.

Planet Earth

Birds winging across the sky,

A baby's heart beating,

Creatures of the night,

The greatest planet of them all.

Dead Planet

Bitter, painful Mother Planet,

Spouting tumbleweed in the desert.

Scorpions, rocks, bones and sage,

All lay lifeless amidst wasteland dirt.

The Mighty Feat

Distant beaches burning

In sun's eternal heat.

But earth absorbs the infinite beauty

Of our Creator's mighty feat.

The Watchers

We, the watchers, look patiently

Toward the stars, heaven, and moon,

Waiting for a miracle resembling peace,

Hopefully soon.

Universal Peace

Planets, Moon, and Sun

All

Rhythmically harmonizing in

Love, Hope, Joy, and

Peace.

Chapter IV

Trials and Tribulations
(But not without hope)

Man Confused

Evolution or creation...

Absolution or dissolution...

Contribution or retribution...

Execution or institution...

Persecution or resolution...

"Humans"! What do we know?

Rewards From Above

Northern lights reflect calm,

Peace, and hope for life's rewards.

With Heaven watching.

Will ye be prepared?

Spiritual Conflict

In this corner.....The Soul

In that corner.....The Body

The referee...Your Conscience

Satan takes the loser

Gentlemen.....Beware!

Changing Fate

Found etchings on stone,

Foretold of man's pending doom.

Shall crumble this stone

To alter its prophecy.

My Prayer

Pray for love and calm,

Keep us safe from harm,

Wait for peace patiently,

Thy will be done certainly.

Amen

Escape to Paradise

Black slave escaping plantation,

Ending years of poverty and sorrow,

Found God's Paradise...

Only by death.

Hallowed Graves

These hallowed unmarked graves,

Each solitary and mute,

Have within them generations

Of a loving past.

Urban Plight

Unlit city nights,

Ghetto streets and roads

Perpetuate urban plights,

Festers then implodes.

Haunting Moments

Haunting moments echoed in my soul.

Stood steadfastly and found

Strength and faith at the

Gates of comfort.

Thing

Invisible, untouchable, shapeless,

And without light.

Such is that mass of unemboweled entity,

The obstinate, unsoul sprite.

Persistence

Life isn't as you wish.

Touch but not feel,

Hurt but not heal,

Look but not see,

Stumbles but persists.

A Beacon of Hope

A beacon of hope,

As far as the eyes could see,

Shimmered and glittered

Across the swirling sea.

Chapter V

Inner Peace
(And not so...)

Be Ready

Always wishing, wanting, begging,

Praying, asking, hoping,

For peace.

Now I truly understand

Part of God's plan.

Must be ready.

The Gatekeepers

Double-headed beast

Looking to end achievements

Of mankind.

'Tis a wonder we are the

Unyielding gatekeepers.

Man's Salvation

Immense machine awoke itself,

Thought man its own creation.

God's wonderful unspoken assurance

Reminded man of his salvation.

Last Meal

Fair play, integrity, incorruptibility:

Ingredients for the last meal

In preparation to achieve immortality.

Fairyland Dreams

Midsummer's warming sun

Surrounding simple happenings,

While perfect day had shone

Of fairyland dreams

Once gone.

Country Dreaming

Passing vertical poles

With suspended telegraph line,

Crossing railroad tracks

With fading whistle wine.

This country dream is mine.

Idle Time

Reward the idle with too much time,

Add more time to a ticking bomb.

'Tis no difference.

Faded Memories

Dreams of colorful rainbows,

Pleasant rhymes and tunes,

Memories of fragile hopes,

All vanish like windswept dunes.

Man on the Moon

Dusty moon drought,

Half side light out,

Yellow cheesy face

Between a rock and a hard place.

Life's Changes

Changes happen in life.

Stay sane and

Conquer personal strife,

For much ado means no peace.

Eternal Life

Love today like no tomorrow,

Eternal life and peace

Shall follow.

Nothing Impossible

Everything everywhere,

From unrestrained to expectations,

Nothing is impossible,

But may unfurl your soul.

Things Happen

Anything and everything...

Peace, calm, harmony,

Strife, love, reward,

And changes

Will certainly happen tonight...

Somewhere.

Time Passing

Time chiming ceaselessly,

With measured, rhythmical beating,

Never to falter or relent,

With each passing moment.

Chapter VI

People
(The good and the bad)

With Love

Mothers and Grandmothers,

Equally,

Have been loving us

Unconditionally.

Time to repay them,

Dutifully.

The Poet

The mighty poet,

Sowing words of mundane,

Transforming ordinary into extraordinary.

A magical gardener is he.

The Sculptor

Sculptor's hands slowly aging,

Reaching his golden years.

Yet to create his masterpiece

And earn acceptance by his peers.

The Old Man and His Fiddle

The old man fiddled quiet notes

Of Mozart's written score,

His hands slowly fading,

Soon the music is no more.

A Friend in Need

Thinking silent thought,

Friendships can be bought.

Try he may, but soon to learn

It fails more often than not.

Woe is Me

Enduring unending tyrant's sting.

Not at all like Heaven,

But life without its woes is

My inevitable death.

Faith Agains the Wicked

Even the mightiest fools bleed,

And death is inevitable,

I have faith against the wicked,

Because God says I'm able.

Struggle For Freedom

My struggle for freedom

Thunders with pride and glory,

But my blade and musket

Shall not be tarnished

With your blood.

Passion for Life

Your evil satanic ways

Are harsh but in vein.

My compassion for life

Is relentless

And forever full of praise.

Hate Monger

Insinuate, instigate,

Cast rumors of untrue,

Spread your hate, discriminate,

Your venom you do spew.

Equality

Judge me not

With your critical review,

I am human,

Just like you.

The Villain Queen

Feasting on sweet bread

Within your ivory tower,

Perfumes and incense of roses red,

Flaunting your rise to power.

Chapter VII

The Curse of War

Where's the Joy

Blood stained waters gurgle,

Haunting dark caverns.

Ancient war-time battle fields,

Tears descending down mountains'

Pathways.

Still looking for joy.

Bleeding Blood

Blood, blood, red blood,

Thick blood bleeding

From wounds on my hands.

Hot blood, sticky blood,

Soaking in the sand.

War

Wasting time waging war,

Raising arms of quest.

Let only the bravest fight

To victory for the oppressed.

The Unknown Soldiers

Motionless bodies lay under sandstone.

Torn and tattered flags wave

O'er aged, weathered headstones.

Nary a name for the brave.

Chapter VIII

Taboos

One Armed Bandit

Insensitive one-armed jackal

Flagrantly prodding hopeless souls'

Eventual demise and fading hopes.

Dreams of Riches

Romanticize and fantasize,

Thoughts of rags to riches,

Sadness turns to madness

With fleeting glamour and glitter.

Friends of Mine

Amassing wealth to large degree,

Achieving goals and means to ends,

Better watch your enemy,

Best to know your friends.

Too Vane

Vane and single fellows

Label themselves immortal.

It's no wonder

After flirts with skirts

The ladies seem to chortle.

Strip Tease

She taunts and teases

With anatomical beauty,

Engaging in flirtatious game.

Has she no shame?

To Each His Own

Fully confused species

Harboring x-rated desirous lifestyle

And rainbow-painted courtship.

My Philosophy

With love in her heart

She is free to be kissed

By black, white, or multicolored.

Her choice.

The Unborn

Dismayed and panicked girl,

Too complacent in aborting

The perfect Love.

Confessing won't do.

Reconsider the life yet born.

Internal Chaos

Splintered, shattered, distressed,

Chaotic feeling of helplessness.

Harboring contemplation

Of mortal emptiness.

Found reassurance with unselfishness.

Self Destruction

Searching within his soul

For an answer simple,

About to lose control

And destroy his body temple.

Desperation

Silhouette of desperate woman

Against the swelling tide.

She contemplates and hesitates

While Satan patiently waits.

Caged Souls

Caged and confined inside concrete places,

Forgotten, restless souls,

Lost their freedom and acceptance,

Their fate... to become sacrificial roles.

Lost Thoughts

Dredging the mind

For gleeting images...

Like laying waste

To one's own backyard.

Anger Management

Fighting anger with desperation,

Unsettling, unable to laugh.

Words of despair go unheard,

By those to act on my behalf.

Misfits

Cross-eyed misfits

With unshaped souls,

Wailing worry tears

As their useless world folds.

Are we not their keepers?

Chapter IX

Odds and Ends
(Leftovers)

Moody People

The Poor somewhat hopeful,

The Admired foolishly sanguine,

Fakers love themselves,

All others whine pathetically.

How sad!

Staying Focused

Looking beyond

The curves of life?

Stay focused

On what's already in sight.

Things I Like

Pancakes, crossword puzzles,

An occasional nip on weekends,

The way a newborn puppy nuzzles,

And poker with my friends.

World History

Criss-crossing the years,

Past, present, future,

Collection of events

Shaping what was, is, and will be.

Red Pony

Lacquered-red pony

With thick, braided mane,

Sniffed my outstretched hands,

Filled with straw, love and sugar cane.

Puzzle Pieces

Misshaped puzzle pieces,

Shapeless, faceless pieces,

Missing corner pieces,

Unfit, leftover pieces.

Broken Glass

Broken ornamental glass

Strewn across the floor,

Shapes forming beautiful lights,

Much ado no more.

Flowers Amongst Weeds

Luscious bright colors

Of landscaped hills,

Flowers growing tall of meadows,

Dancing about in endless fields

Amongst the cannabis shadows.

Book of Knowledge

Yellowed faded dog-eared pages,

Battered spine and tattered edges,

Collecting dust since ancient ages,

Lots of knowledged still it cages.

Sea of Cees

Children consuming cookies,

Couples coping cancerous cigarettes,

Clients came calling

Combining careful criticisms,

Can't collect city charges.

Case closed.

Comfort Zone

ATM's, grocery lines,

Waiting for the phone,

Don't be afraid,

I mean you no harm,

I respect your comfort zone.

Subway

Subway coaches under city street,

Hustling, whizzing, screeching,

Through cavernous darkness,

Like wind of fleet

Enroute to farthest reaching.

Gotta Go

Strolling on the beach at night,

Guided by full moonlight,

Answering nature's calling,

Passing on shore edge surging.

Judgement Day

Now's the time to declare

Your right as a citizen,

Because fast approaching

Is judgement day,

Aka April fifteen.

Street Mime

Running hard, still in place,

Abstract gaze upon his face,

Looks confused, lost in time,

Bewildered life, street corner mime.

Wet T-Shirt

Arms are really hanging down,

Heavily hung in body sweat,

Inside out, down and crumpled,

Wearing t-shirt dripping wet.

The Hands of Angels

At the hands of Angels

Birds fly free,

Boys climb tree,

Politicians agree to disagree,

Two in love become three.

My Best

Unmeaning words have no depth,

Silly rhymes dismay me.

Unfortunately, this is my best,

Until next time...maybe.

The End